To Be A Good Man

STEPHEN MERRITT, JR

2026 To Be A Good Man
By: Stephen Merritt, Jr.

Published by:

CoolBird Publishing House
Birmingham, Alabama 35243
www.CoolBirdPublishingHouse.com

ISBN: 979-8-234-11560-7

Printed in the United States of America.
First Edition – 2026

COOLBIRD
PUBLISHING
HOUSE™

Dedication

This book is dedicated to my children: Savanna, Stephen III (Trace), and Preston. I have always strived to be an example to you, showing that it is possible to live for God without ever compromising your faith, integrity, or morals. Always be mindful of the company you keep, the impression you leave on others, and the influence you allow others to have on you.

-Dad

Table of Contents

Foreword

When I think about my husband, I don't just think about the man he is today. I think about the journey it took for him to become that man. I think about the experiences that tested him, the people who poured into him, the mistakes he learned from, and the moments that could have broken him but instead helped shape him. I think about the way God kept His hand on his life through every season... even the hard ones. This book is personal; Not because it tells a perfect story, but because it tells a real one. The man writing these pages is someone who has lived through pain, growth, disappointment, love, lessons, and transformation. He's a man who has been impacted by the guidance of other men throughout his life... some who encouraged him, some who challenged him, and some who simply showed up at the right time when he needed direction most. As his wife, I've had the privilege of seeing the parts of him most people don't. I've seen his strength, but I've also seen his vulnerability. I've seen his faith carry him through moments when giving up would have been easier. I've watched him work to become not just a better man for himself, but a better husband, father, and example for others. What I love most about this book is that it doesn't pretend to have all the answers. It simply tells the truth. And sometimes the truth is the most powerful thing a person can offer. My prayer is that, as you read these pages, you find something that speaks to you... whether it’s encouragement, reflection, healing, motivation, or simply a reminder that God can use every part of our story for something greater. Thank you for taking the time to read his story. I know it wasn’t easy to write, and I truly believe someone will be changed because he did.

... Portia Merritt

Introduction

Honestly, I don't know how to begin this book. I'm not sure at what point in your life you suddenly become aware that something needs to change. You begin to question yourself, life, and the world. You start to second-guess the things you've been taught and become aware of the advice you took that you shouldn't have. You begin to feel a weight on your shoulders that wasn't there before... the heaviness of your wrong decisions, the sting of the opportunities you missed, and the arrogance of bad habits that told you that you can't live without them. How do we combat these things? How do we gain strength without ego, confidence without pride, and show kindness without being taken advantage of? How do we become the man necessary to carry the weight of family and life's responsibilities without becoming someone we can't look at in the mirror?

A lot of these answers we tend to seek from a father or some father figure who stood in that position when our father wasn't there, like a coach or teacher, maybe even your favorite athlete or artist. A wise man once told me that we are the children of whomever's instructions we obey. Which explains why Jesus did not take heed to Satan when he suggested that He should fall down and worship him or throw Himself off the mountain. Jesus alway s responded with what His Father told Him... that we should trust the Lord our God and Him alone. Whether we know it or not, we all follow the commands of our father. We all take heed to the voice that we recognize, respect, or the one that speaks the loudest. Whomever's instructions we obey, that is our father.

As men, God designed us to seek our Father for direction, advice, and the skills necessary to navigate the environment we live in. A father passes down the tools he learned on his journey, and even some he picked up from his father, and so on and so on... some good, some not. We receive those tools consciously and subconsciously. For example, my father taught me never to hit a woman, to always open her door, pay for dinner, and so on. That's what I did. On the other hand, I found myself treating women the way I heard about through music... hip hop mostly. You know, "love 'em and leave 'em," "bros before hoes," "f women, get money." If you listen to hip hop, I'm sure you know what I'm talking about. It all sounded good, but it was trash, and my life began to reflect that. There came a point where I noticed the impact the men around me had on my life. I would do or say something, and it would remind me of someone I knew or something I'd heard. I was becoming who I gave my attention to and received counsel from. The guys I hung around, the music I listened to, and the movies I'd watched... it was all molding me, shaping me into the man I was becoming. I moved out of my parents' home and joined the military at 18. You would think that I would learn discipline, honor, self-respect, integrity, and maybe even continue in the Christian foundation my parents set for me. Honestly, I feel like I was worse coming out of the Army than when I went in. Because I didn't have much male guidance in the military, I stayed high and drunk, partied, chased and slept with women who were single, married, old, and young. I've stolen cars, broken into houses and pawned what I found, gone to jail for writing hot checks, and received several DUI charges while underage... all while serving in the military.

Being so far from home, I had grown frustrated with making bad decisions, seeing the disappointment on my mother's face whenever I saw her, and feeling like I was purposed for more than I was, but I didn't know how to turn things around.
I remember sitting on the edge of my bed in my underwear, looking at myself in the mirror. I asked God to show me. To remove everything in me that wasn't like Him. From that moment, I began to see myself for who I was, and I didn't like it. I saw my failures as a son, the disappointment in the eyes of women I truly cared about, and the discouragement of only seeing a glimpse of the soldier I once desired to become. I had fallen, and up until that point, everything I had decided to cling to was slowly destroying the man I wanted to be.

Once I was discharged from active duty, I felt lost. I tried to incorporate what I did receive from the military... the discipline, confidence, and relentlessness to keep moving forward in spite of obstacles. While trying to find and rebuild myself, I bought a Bible and read... religiously (lol, ikr). From the time I woke up until the time I went to sleep, I was in the Word. At work during break, lunch, second break, and even during downtime, I was in the Word. Similar to how we treat our cell phones now, that's how I was with the Word of God. He began to father me through His Word. Through the process of time, God has been opening my eyes. I see the relationships I have and the people and things I interact with differently. Did you know that most people possess God-like qualities and don't even know it? Confidence, consistency, patience, kindness, charity, wanting equality and justice, standing up for the oppressed and protecting the innocent, being honorable, and speaking the truth in love. The ability to plan, stay focused, keep your word, and walk in integrity... all these are what the Bible calls good. These qualities may be handled selfishly, misdirected, or misused, but the attributes themselves are still good. Most people already possess some of these qualities, and in reading the Bible, I noticed the good qualities of the people I crossed paths with. I started implementing them in my own life.

This book is a collection of things I learned from the men around me, some habits I picked up from them, and some that I found within myself. Anything in me that God did not call good, I began to throw off because it wasn't conducive to the man I wanted to be. Hopefully, this book will encourage you to examine yourself and the people you associate with. What are they teaching you? What habits, good or bad, do the people around you possess that you now find within yourself? My goal for the men who read this book is to become more conscious of who they surround themselves with and make adjustments according to the man they want to become.

-Stephen

Chapter 1 - Big Steve

"Love is patient, love is kind. It does not envy; it does not boast; it is not proud. It does not dishonor others, it is not self-seeking, it is not easily angered, and it keeps no record of wrongs. Love does not delight in evil but rejoices with the truth. It always protects, always trusts, always hopes, and always perseveres." 1 Corinthians 13:4-7

When speaking on the impact that men have made on my life, it is only right that I start with my dad. There are many things I pulled from him. His consistency in showing up for every major part of my life is a big one for me. While he and my mom divorced when I was a toddler, I've always remembered him being present. I lived with my mom and stepdad, so every summer and for some holidays, he and one of his childhood friends would make that hour-plus ride from New Orleans to Amite, LA, to pick me up. As I got older, he was at my high school graduation and Army basic training graduation in Ft. Knox, KY. He visited me at my first duty station in Ft. Hood, TX. He was there for my wedding, and at every home I have lived in, from LA to MS to TX, he always showed up.

As a son, that means a lot to me, and it is part of my character toward my children and the people I love. I try to show up. "I love you, Bruh" is something I often hear from my dad. It happened so much that I remember asking him why he always told me that. He said that as a child, he never heard that from his father. He had never heard his father tell him that he loved him. He would go on to tell me he never really spent time with his dad and rarely ever saw him. I wonder, where does a man who never had a relationship with his father learn how to be one? Where did he learn to show up or feel the need to consistently remind me that he loves me or that he will always be there for me? Is it because he never had that? Did not experiencing those things leave a scar that he didn't want me to bear? I hear many stories of people being one way because their father was that way, or not because of the same reason. Their father was an alcoholic, so they're an alcoholic. Or their father was an alcoholic, so they don't touch the stuff.

It's up to us to decide whether we will continue the toxic behaviors we witness from others or change the narrative. My dad never heard "I love you" from his dad, so he always told me he loved me, and so I tell my children I love them all the time. My dad changed the standard of the Merritt men in his lineage with three words. There are many more things I learned from him. Being married three times, I've never heard him speak negatively toward his exes. To me about my mom or to my little brother about his, no matter what the situation was. He would say his piece, whether we understood where he was coming from or not, and he would leave it at that.

I've seen him redirect the verbal abuse of a mother toward her child onto himself. He would make light of a hostile situation so that the aggressor would either laugh or turn their attack onto him. I've witnessed him do that countless times, and it reminded me of this verse in Proverbs 15: "A soft answer turns away wrath, but a harsh word stirs up anger." Learning to control your emotions is something every man should learn to master. Not allowing outside influences to determine your response or reacting out of feelings can save your life, your marriage, and your relationships with your kids or business partners. That lesson alone changed the way I respond to adversity of all kinds. Speak calmly when temperatures are high and watch the climate shift. It's almost like a superpower. We are not created to “match the energy” presented to us but to change the atmosphere entirely.

My dad is still there for me whenever I need him. One thing I often call him for is when I’m having vehicle trouble. He taught me how to maintain any vehicle I’ve ever owned and gave me the confidence to deal with any situation I’ve come across. One of his most memorable quotes that I use in many areas of my life is, “If something is in your way, move it.” I know he was speaking of when I’m replacing parts on my car, but it’s good advice when I face fear, anxiety, depression, or whatever the obstacle may be. If something is stopping me from moving forward in relationships, in business, or in life in general, push through it, move it, whatever... but don’t let it stop you from doing what you need to do.

Chapter 2 - Joe

"Train up a child in the way they should go, and when he is older he will not depart from it." Proverbs 22:6

"And to aspire to live quietly, and to mind your own business, and work with your hands, as we instructed you, so that you may walk properly before outsiders and be dependant on no one." Thessalonians 4:11-12

I've always believed a man who brings another man's child into his home and raises them as his own deserves some level of respect, even if it's just for that. For whatever reason, my mother and father split when I was a toddler. Both remarried and started anew, and I lived primarily with my mother. From what I remember, Christianity was our practice. We learned of the Trinity and the laws and ways of God. As far as I can remember, my stepdad referred to me as his son, not stepson. (I'm only referring to him as my stepdad for the sake of this writing.) His approach to raising me was preceded by his father, a man we called PawPaw, who I know was a major inspiration for who he is as a man. My stepdad raised us with a stern hand. His yes was yes, and his no was no.

From him, I learned the value of hard work. His approach to me failing a class was yard work. "If you don't want to learn in school, then manual labor is what you'll be left with, so you might as well get used to it," is what he would say. Needless to say, I never failed a grade. One of my life mantras is, "You eat the meat and spit out the bones." I say that because in every relationship, I tend to adopt what benefits me and discard what doesn't, making adjustments here and there. My stepdad was a great example of a working man, but it's bittersweet because that's all he did. He didn't make it to my high school graduation, basic training graduation, wedding, the births of my children, birthdays, or holidays, and I only remember him visiting one of the many places I've lived.

Please don't get me wrong. I don't feel any resentment toward him for any of it. People are who they are, and like his father, he's not that type of man. I know his love for me is genuine, and the foundation in the Word of God he set for me is a major part of my development. I just fear that when he comes to the end of his days and looks back on life, he may find that he did not truly live. Although my stepdad wasn't there for those highlighted moments in my life or the lives of my siblings, I don't believe it was because he didn't care. People tend to show love in different ways, and for him, it was providing. To make sure our home had its foundation in God and a roof over our heads. Watching him, I learned the power of having a vision and preparing for it. I watched him enjoy the shade today from a tree that he planted when I was a child, and I saw the end result of something that took 30 years to materialize.
How many of us can say we have that level of foresight? Can you see the end from the beginning? Do you have a plan, and will you dedicate your time, energy, resources, and life to seeing it come to fruition? How important to you is the manifestation of your vision or purpose? Who benefits from it?

God put a purpose in my stepfather that he dedicated his life to completing. Whatever is going on in this world didn't seem to distract him from what he set his mind to do. We should all have that same mindset... to complete the work God has put in our hearts to do. I'd be lying if I said it didn't have an effect on me, having these moments and him not witnessing his prayers for me coming true. There was a longing to see him there, to see him smile, and witness the goodness of God in my life. One thing I know my stepfather did was pray for me. We used to have family prayer often when I was a child, and I've even implemented it into my own family. I understand there is power in prayer, and much of what I've accomplished is because of the prayers of my parents. The memories of waking up in the middle of the night to a parent crying out to God imprinted a standard of parenthood within me. It showed me what was necessary for today's battles and tomorrow's challenges.

Being present in your children's favorite memories is one of the greatest feelings a parent can experience. Most times, just being there is the highlight and not the situation itself. Growing up, my mom introduced us to "The Dark Game," where we would try to find specific items in the house or each other in the dark. It was one of the most iconic games of my childhood. We didn't realize it until we got older, but during those times, we had no electricity in our house... not because it wasn't available, it just wasn't available to us. That is a core memory for me because my mom was there. She made the most of a hard situation, so much so that I never saw it as a bad thing when we didn't have power. I saw it as an opportunity to play "The Dark Game."

Chapter 3 - Sgt Woods

"Do not be afraid of their faces, for I am with you to deliver you, says the Lord." Jeremiah 1:8

"With the Lord's authority I say this: Live no longer as the Gentiles do, for they are hopelessly confused. Their minds are full of darkness; they wander far from the life God gives them because they have closed their minds and hardened their hearts against Him. They have no sense of shame. They live for lustful pleasure and eagerly practice every kind of impurity." - Ephesians 4:17-19

When I transitioned out of the Army, I went into the National Guard, stationed in New Orleans. Still in my mannish ways, I remember standing in a circle with some other guys in my unit. Our conversations were usually about "Who's the best MC: Biggie, Jay-Z, or Nas?" Lil Wayne lyrics, and women in the unit we wouldn't mind sleeping with. Once, during one of our usual cyphers, Sgt. Woods walked into the middle of our circle and asked, "If you were to die right now, where do you think you would go, Heaven or Hell?" Me, growing up in the church, quickly replied, "Nobody knows. Only God knows where we are going." He replied, "If you don't KNOW, then you're going to Hell," and he turned around and walked off. I was furious. How is he gonna tell me I'm going to Hell? He doesn't know me. That weighed on me for the rest of the day. Was I really going to Hell? Who does he think he is, telling me that? I'm saved, right? I mean, I grew up in church. I was baptized when I was little, so... I'm good, right? Wrong.

Galatians 5:19 tells us, *"The acts of the flesh are obvious: adultery, fornication, impurity and debauchery; idolatry and witchcraft; hatred, discord, jealousy, fits of rage, selfish ambition, dissensions, factions and envy; murders and drunkenness; orgies, and the like. I warn you, as I did before, that those who live like this will not inherit the kingdom of God."*

I believe that encounter is what opened my eyes to my own reality. I pretty much checked all those boxes. I was lost. I needed to know that I was good with God. At that point, I really didn't care about anything else. I needed to get myself together. After that encounter with Sgt. Woods, my priorities shifted, but my environment didn't. If you know anything about New Orleans, most of what's celebrated... the food, festivals, music, tourist attractions, foreign arts, and architecture... is seasoned with mixes of Christianity, Catholicism, and voodoo practices. If you are not careful, you can easily get lost in the beauty and excitement of the city. I thank God for Sgt. Woods. Years passed before I realized how far I was from God and how much his words had meant to me.

What I once thought was harsh and insensitive, I now see was all love. That situation taught me this: Truth is not optional, even when it is uncomfortable. I wonder how long he wrestled with telling us that. How difficult was it for Sgt. Woods to walk into a circle of grown men and speak what God told him to say? And to say that if we are unsure of our eternal destination, then we are bound for Hell. Truth is, no conscious adult ends up in Heaven by accident. It takes an intentional pursuit to know God, learn of and accept His Son Jesus as the only sacrifice for your sin, in order to enter those gates. If you knowingly live your life in obedience to God, then there is no question where you're headed.

Chapter 4 - C. Rose

"Brothers, if any man be overtaken in a fault, you who are spiritual, restore such a one in the spirit of meekness; considering yourself lest you also be tempted."- Galatians 6:1

"A good man out of the good treasure of his heart brings forth that which is good; and the evil man out of the evil treasure of his heart brings forth that which is evil; for out of the abundance of the hearth the mouth speaks." -Luke 6:45

In 2004, around the time I had that encounter with Sgt. Woods, I was working at the Walmart Distribution Center. With the understanding that I needed to make some life changes, I began to seek God about everything. It's one thing when people tell you what God requires, but it's another when your heart changes or you cross paths with people who speak to you the very things you've been praying about in secret. Being newly saved and still trying to work out my salvation, I was learning what it meant to be a child of God. I wasn't sure what it actually looked like. What about me was good or bad? How should I feel about the world around me or interact with it? Everything felt new. I was aware that there were some things I had to let go of... getting high and drunk, maybe even chasing women. One of the first things the Holy Spirit began to convict me of was music.

I was a great fan of hip-hop music. I loved the creativity of it. The ability to express yourself with words in rhythmic form is something that I've always had a thing for. I had two CD books full of artists that I'd listen to religiously and had committed most of their lyrics to memory. In the midst of my faith walk, both my CD cases were stolen. I replaced them all, plus some,

and they were stolen again. I figured this was a sign that I needed to give them up, so I accepted that this was God's doing and moved on. Before I got saved, I was the guy who rapped all the lyrics to my favorite music to myself... OUT LOUD. All street, all gangster, all drugs, women, and money all the time. I never really told my coworkers about my newfound faith, but when you're rapping Jay-Z one minute and singing Fred Hammond the next, it starts to raise some eyebrows.
One day, while riding through the warehouse, a guy by the name of C. Rose, who was about my age, rode up on a pallet jack and said, "Whatchu gonna do, Steve? You're gonna have to pick one, man. Is it gonna be God or this world? You gotta pick one."

I laughed it off, but that stuck with me. *"Choose this day whom you will serve..."* is the partial verse that repeated in my head. From that time on, I would find and speak with C. Rose about God, the Bible, Jesus, and whatever else I had questions about. He answered what he could but always insisted that I buy myself a Bible, and so I did. Buying a Bible and reading it for myself, I would replace my old music with Scripture. Reading consistently enabled me to retain much of what I read. Oftentimes the old music still crept up, and before long I was rapping Biggie again.

It was a struggle for me not to associate my life with a rap song, and it took years for me to purge many song lyrics from my everyday speech. Being consistent with reading the Bible helped me tremendously in replacing my thoughts with Scripture, and over time I just stopped thinking of them. I never knew C. Rose to be a believer before that first interaction with him. Not because he didn't carry himself as one, but because I wasn't looking for Christians. Also, he wasn't pushing his beliefs on random people, "evangelizing," "judging," or preaching to people. He was attentive, listening for the voice of God or the nudge of the Holy Spirit, and he was available. As men, we must always be aware of our surroundings... whether it's the people we work with or the situations we find ourselves in. Make it your business to pay attention to what's going on and learn to read the room. Doing so may provide an opportunity to encourage someone, a chance to protect those you love, or even open a door that God has set before you. There is a passage that tells us not to cast our pearls before swine. I understand that to mean don't give what is valuable to people who won't appreciate it or who would trample it. I found later in my walk how draining it is to try to spread the gospel to people who could care less. It is much easier to share with those who seek after what I am willing to give.

C. Rose was attentive to those around him. I believe he was sensitive to the voice of the Holy Spirit and moved at the right moment when I gave him the opportunity. Those few words he spoke remind me to this day to be mindful of whom I serve. Since the mouth speaks what the heart is full of, I understand now that what I continuously recite may reveal what is still in me that hasn't been dealt with. That brother watered me, and I thank God for him. Over the course of several months of talking with C. Rose and finally buying a Bible, I binge-read, and it was great. On my 45-minute commute to and from work, I needed something to listen to. I had given up all the secular records that I owned and didn't have anything to replace them with.

During one of our powwows, I was telling C. Rose about it and was surprised to learn that he also loved hip-hop. In his music, the artists rapped about God. There were artists out there making music about sharing the gospel, theology, and their own walk with God. I had never heard of that before and was ecstatic, to say the least. Over time, I began to fill my music catalog with people whom I felt represented the Christ I was longing to know... the One whom I read about in the pages of the Bible I had grown to love. If you are like me and enjoy hip-hop music, here are a few artists that I've grown to enjoy over the years:

- Eshon Burgundy
- Bizzle
- HezekiYah
- Gemstones
- Paisley the Hebrew
- Jackie Hill Perry
- Gifted Hands
- Alano Adan
- J. Monty
- Sevin
- Lathan Warlick
- Andy Mineo
- Laynell Grant
- Dee-1
- Indy Tribe
- Kalam Montgomery
- Young Noah, Aable, and Callhimd

Chapter 5 - Brown

"Likewise, the tongue is a small part of the body, but it makes great boasts. Consider what a great forest is set on fire by a small spark. The tongue also is a fire, a world of evil among the parts of the body. It corrupts the whole body, sets the whole course of one's life on fire, and is itself set on fire by hell." - James 3:5-6

"With the tongue we praise our Lord and Father, and with it we curse human beings, who have been made in God's likeness. Out of the same mouth comes praise and cursing. My brothers and sisters, this should not be. Can both fresh water and saltwater flow from the same spring? My brothers and sisters, can a fig tree bear olives or a grapevine bear figs? Neither can a salt spring produce fresh water." -James 3:9-12

When I reflect on the people who impacted my life, Brown is always at the top of the list. We served in the National Guard together, and he was right there in the circle when Sgt. Woods dropped his "y'all going to Hell" bombshell. Brown always stood out because he didn't curse. It was a small detail that was mostly overlooked, but I found it intriguing. He was a professing Christian, and while I didn't know the depth of his walk, that one discipline stayed with me. Eventually, I decided to try it too.

The Sgt. Woods incident was the catalyst I needed to actually change. I began to treat my speech like a game, trying to think before I spoke. It was a massive challenge; profanity was my native tongue. It was exactly how I expressed myself. For a time, I felt lost... I didn't know any other words that carried the same weight. I was reminded of the times I stood before my parents. The respect I have for them never allowed those words to escape my mouth. The self-control was already there; I just had to harness it. The Bible speaks of being slow to speak and quick to listen, so I began to weigh my words and my answers to questions before I spoke. I learned that what you give your attention to shapes who you are... how you act, respond, and conduct yourself. I became mindful of the books I read, the music I listened to, and the movies I watched. Those small changes began to reshape the way I saw the world. Before long, I no longer struggled to "watch my mouth" because foul language was no longer part of my vocabulary. As the saying goes, "Out of the abundance of the heart the mouth speaks." My words were being purified because my heart was being purified. That small rudder set the course for a new direction in my life, and I was finally ready for the journey ahead.

Chapter 6 - Eshon

"In this the children of God and the children of the devil are manifest: Whoever does not practice righteousness is not of God, nor is he who does not love his brother." 1 John 3:10
"For as many are led by the Spirit of God, these are the sons of God." Romans 8:14

When I was younger, rap music wasn't allowed in our house; my parents didn't want to hear it at all. The belief that rap is "from the devil" is one held by many, not just Christians... and understandably so. Much of what has been presented to us, from lessons on quick money to fast cars and faster lifestyles, supports that view. Growing up in an impoverished area, I saw how rap was used as a blueprint for "rags to riches," serving as a manual for survival, often favoring illegal paths over legal ones. I've often said that what you give your attention to... friends, family, or entertainment... shapes your character. When I was "coming out of the world," one of the hardest things to give up was my CD collection. My love for hip-hop wasn't rooted in the lifestyle it glorified, but in the artistry... the patterns, the cadences, and the poetic expression of a shared struggle. However, a day came when that music could no longer sustain me. My spirit became vexed by the very songs that once mirrored my life.

The shift happened when the music no longer satisfied me. When I listened to the records that had shaped the man I was up to that point, my spirit became vexed. I could no longer relate to the words; they weren't sufficient for the path ahead. Truthfully, it saddened and excited me at the same time. I was sad to walk away from what I loved, but excited because I knew I wasn't doing this on my own. No one told me I had to give it up... it was God. This was proof that He was listening to my prayers. In letting go, I realized how rap can be a powerful force used by the enemy to manipulate through the "carrots" of money and power. Whether as a creator or a listener, its hook has led many toward jail or the grave, trapped by the mantra to "live fast and die young."

With my newfound taste for music that edified my spirit and glorified God, I stumbled upon Eshon Burgundy... a Christian rap artist. Before then, I had rarely heard anyone rap about God, and when I did, it felt corny. As someone who respects artistry, wordplay, and production, Christian rap usually didn't make the cut. To me, it felt like going from the profound works of Maya Angelou and Langston Hughes to Dr. Seuss with a few "Jesus" and "Bible" references thrown in. I just couldn't do it. However, everything changed when I heard his song "I Don't Want You." He writes:

"The Prince of the Air" wants to get me twisted, offer me everything that he has been made rich with but then I flashed the wedding ring that's wrapped around my spirit, this matrimony is not only wrapped around my lyrics, it's wrapped around my heart, I rap it just so you can hear it, in fact it's my armor, this what happens when I wear it happily married to the UNIVERSAL ENGINEER, DESIGNER of that refining fire let's make it clear, ALPHA comma OMEGA comma THE PIONEER So Lucifer ay boy I'm stepping out the crew, you keep trying to make me murder GOD is trying to take me further HE could redefine a man I understand, I'm living proof so now I . . . I don't want you."

Songs like this and many others by Eshon were played on repeat literally every day for years. In every stage of my walk in Christ, when feasting on the Word of God, his music became the seasoning that allowed me to marinate on what I had ingested. Just like when I was in the world and rap shaped my former man, God broke that mold and used it to reshape the man I am today. I learned how to walk in the love, peace, and conviction of God while listening to his music. His words resonated with my spirit because in them I could see my own struggles, victories, frustrations, and sometimes doubt. All of it is expressed through his music.
Even though I've never met him in person, I can hear his growth as a man, as a husband, father, and believer. The Word of God has a way of connecting strangers and making them siblings. We have different parents, but because we obey the Word of God, we share a Father. I can know you without knowing you. I can trust you without ever meeting you, and through your own actions, believers can tell if you've been with Jesus. My collection of music was the first of many areas of my life that God pulled me away from. The lifestyle it glorified was full of every type of sin, evil, and wickedness you could think of; it was designed that way. It made sin look so cool. It normalized it, and the consequences of it are the foundational plight of many people, especially people of color.

We don't realize how effective music is in our lives and how we become the living embodiment of what we listen to. Just as Jesus is God's Word manifested in the flesh, we can become the lies and thoughts of Satan and manifest them in our own lives. Our behavior shows us who our father is. It is a direct reflection of who we obey and disobey. John 8 reads that we all share the desires of our father. If you desire righteousness, it's because God, your Heavenly Father, is righteous. If your desires are carnal and sinful, if you seek to do evil and wickedness in this life, it is because your father is just that.

When you look at those whom you attach yourself to, whom you follow, and those to whom you give access to your mind through music, movies, or whatever else, who do you see? When you recognize the character of a person, you can see who their spiritual father is. You can see who's leading them. Is that who you want to follow? Where do you think they are leading you? Is that where you want to go?

(Quick Thought)

What if the follow button on social media is more powerful than we think? Do we proclaim out of our own mouths, "I follow such and such," not realizing how powerful our words are and that we will give an account of every idle word we speak?

When we recite lyrics from these songs, we are coming into agreement with the spirit behind those words. If we are created in the image of God and God creates through the words of His mouth, why do we not think we do the same?

There is a reason God tells us not to practice idle babbling or vain talk, even in prayer. "Wise people will store up knowledge, but the mouth of fools is near destruction." Words have power, and unfortunately, through rap music, people are wielding that power aimlessly, carelessly, in ignorance, and to their own detriment. Oftentimes, I still recite lyrics from songs I haven't heard in years. I have to catch myself and repent of what I said. This was difficult in the beginning because carnal songs were still fresh in my mind. Now, the Holy Spirit catches it before I can even think about it. I pray my musical palate is cleansed through the Word of God so that I neither desire nor am able to tolerate anything outside of that.

Chapter 7 - Obie

"And David shepherded them with integrity of heart; with skillful hands, he led them." -Psalm 78:72

"To do what is right and just is more acceptable to the Lord than sacrifice." -Psalm 21:3

"A friend loves at all times, and a brother is born for adversity." -Proverbs 17:17

"One who has unreliable friends soon comes to ruin, but there is a friend who sticks closer than a brother." -Proverbs 18:24

When I landed at Ft. Hood in '98 as a 19K tanker, Obie was my loader. He'd already put in years at the unit and quickly became my unofficial guide, teaching me who to trust and who to dodge. Funny enough, he was the same guy others warned me to avoid. It didn't take long to see why. Obie was a problem for anyone who opposed logic... or anyone who let him eat chocolate. He was a brilliant, stand-up guy with a serious "Dennis the Menace" streak. He could be a loyal, trusted brother willing to do anything for you, or he could be something like the Taliban, willing to do anything to you, depending on what the situation called for. After serving two and a half years together at Ft. Hood... including a tour in Kuwait... Obie's time in the military came to an end. Before leaving, every soldier is required to go through ACAP, which involves returning all issued equipment (TA-50). If your gear isn't accounted for, your out-processing stops dead in its tracks. Obie was missing several items, so he "borrowed" what he needed from me, though I didn't realize it was more of a donation. Before he left Texas, he apologized for the misunderstanding and promised he'd make it up to me someday.

When my turn to out-process came a few months later, I was the one facing a massive statement of charges. I spent my final weeks "confiscating" any unsecured equipment I found lying around the base. Needless to say, I came up with everything I needed to clear the Army and start my life as a civilian.

Fast forward to 2009... nine years after my discharge... Obie found me on Facebook. He told me he'd been looking for me but simply had no way to get in touch. After we spent some time catching up on the last decade, Obie said, "Bruh, I didn't forget about you," and offered me a job in Arkansas, two states away. I was at a breaking point: a newlywed with a one-year-old and newborn twins, grinding away at a shipyard for low wages and a weekly $375 auto-pay garnishment for a car with a bad transmission. I was stuck. I didn't even have the $60 bus fare to get to the job, which was nine hours away. Obie didn't just pay for my ticket; he invited me into his three-bedroom home to live with his family of five until I could get on my feet. My only challenge was convincing my wife this was a good idea.

"I'm leaving you with three infants to go live with a guy I knew in the Army ten years ago." That was a hard sell, and it was one of the most terrifying decisions I've ever made, but I went. Obie and his family welcomed me with open arms. I stayed for a couple of months, saved every cent, and eventually moved my family from Louisiana into a place of our own. Obie took me on several jobsites after that. Starting from the bottom, I watched how he handled his team with dignity and respect. I witnessed upper management try to ostracize him because he didn't lead with an iron fist, but rather with a heart for his people. As a result, he lost so-called friends and faced missed job opportunities that added stress to his home life. Yet, he stayed

the course. Scripture tells us that "a good name is more desirable than great riches." He understood what I eventually learned: that people are the most precious commodity... far more valuable than money. People can get you into places where money cannot, and they never forget how you treat them. If you treat them well... especially those who can do nothing for you... that seeds a harvest that eventually comes back to you. Today, Obie is thriving in a position far better than the one they tried to keep him in, and he did it without compromising his integrity. God used him and his family to bless mine for years to come, and I will always honor them for it.

Chapter 8 - Ced

"But in your hearts revere Christ as Lord. Always be prepared to give an answer to everyone who asks you to give the reason for the hope that you have. But do this with gentleness and respect, keeping a clear conscience, so that those who speak maliciously against your good behavior in Christ may be ashamed of their slander." -1 Peter 3:15-16

"As I urged you when I went into Macedonia... remain in Ephesus that you may [a]charge some that they teach no other doctrine, nor give heed to fables and endless genealogies, which cause disputes rather than godly edification which is in faith. Now the purpose of the commandment is love from a pure heart, from a good conscience, and from [b]sincere faith, from which some, having strayed, have turned aside to idle talk, desiring to be teachers of the law, understanding neither what they say nor the things which they affirm." -1 Timothy 1:3-7

Ced is my brother-in-law. He has the natural ability to lead people without even trying. By nature, he can be loud, assertive, and authoritative... attributes I've never seen as negative. When used correctly, those traits have a vital place in the Kingdom. I always admired his confidence in what he did, what he said, and how he moved. Personally, I don't naturally possess that same level of self-assurance... that ability to make you believe something is true simply because he said it was.

We both grew up with a Christian background; his grandparents were God-fearing, respectable people. As time passed and the internet made information more accessible, we both began to notice discrepancies between the Bible, history, and what we had been taught in school and church. However, we approached our search for understanding from different perspectives, and at one point, we arrived at very different conclusions.

Whenever we got together, it was like a meeting of the minds; I actually looked forward to those moments. We would dive into history as it pertains to Black Americans, exploring how we became Christians and our ancestral relationship to Egypt. We tackled the heavy claims... arguments like "Christianity is the white man's religion" or "We were kings forced into religion by slave masters." While I won't rehash the details of those debates now, I will say this: our disagreements didn't push me away from my faith. Instead, they drove me into a deeper, more intentional study of the Word of God.

To me, the Bible IS the Truth. Whenever I come across information that seems to contradict it, my first step is prayer: "Lord, give me understanding," then I dive into the text itself. I have realized that much of what is taught from the pulpit or spread through social media is tradition rather than Scripture. Popular quotes like "God gives His toughest battles to His strongest soldiers," "We're all God's children," and "Follow your heart" are just a few that sound good but are not based on Scripture. It's vital to read it for yourself, let the Holy Spirit give you understanding, and seek counsel from those you know are living the Word rather than relying solely on a preacher or the arguments of people who have never studied it.

I can't say for sure what Ced's methods were, but it often seemed like the outside sources he pulled from were more credible to him than the Bible. My stance remained firm: the Bible is God's Word, Jesus is His Son, and access to Heaven is found only through repentance and the acceptance of His sacrifice. I also challenged the narrative; since the people and events of the Bible took place in and around Africa, Christianity being merely a “white man’s religion” is historically not possible.

Those conversations with Ced taught me this: I didn’t know the Word of God as well as I thought. He made great points in showing me that the so-called Black people in the Americas are not being told the whole truth about who we are as a people, where we came from, or the history behind how we got here mentally, physically, or spiritually.

We are lost, looking for answers in anything that makes us see ourselves as more than the oppression we’ve been traumatized with. Looking at our skin color, horoscopes and zodiac signs, fraternities, sororities, or even street gangs... most of which Scripture has labeled witchcraft or demonic... we search for identity. We are pulled in by these things because we have not known God or have forgotten His ways. It made me read and search for understanding in His Word. The current state of our culture isn’t a coincidence; it is the consequence of forsaking the commandments of God. Throughout the Bible, we see a pattern where one generation was responsible for teaching the next about our God... His character, His precepts, and His ways. They were taught the blessings of obedience and the heavy price of rebellion.

Throughout the Old Testament, the Israelites consistently rebelled against God. It only took one generation in which the people did not teach their children the knowledge of God for the whole nation to turn their hearts away from Him. After the Roman destruction of Jerusalem in 70 AD, some “Jews” fled north into areas of Europe, Rome, Greece, and Germany, while many fled into regions of Africa, from Egypt as far as the West Slave Coast. Even now, groups in Ghana, Nigeria, Benin, and

Southern Africa have maintained long-standing Jewish traditions and customs, including feast days and Sabbath rest. Our journey away from God and the consequences of our rebellion can be found in Scripture. Deuteronomy 28:15–68 outlines the specific consequences the Israelites would face for turning away from God's laws. The final verse of that chapter, verse 68, reads:

"And the Lord will take you back to Egypt in ships... there you shall be offered for sale to your enemies...but no man shall redeem you."

I invite you to study these verses for yourself. As you read, consider the timeline of history and ask: Which people have lived out these very words? Our history was stolen or whitewashed, so we lost that foundation. Now, we are operating without a compass, following the ways of a world that prioritizes greed and power over righteousness in a system that wasn't built for the people of God, all while disconnected from Him. By reclaiming our past and understanding why we have been reduced to a byword, we can repent of our former ways, accept the sacrifice of Jesus, and return to the path He originally set for us. By keeping the Bible as my foundation, I've realized that man's truth is a moving target, but God's truth is an anchor. While our perspectives and self-identities evolve over time, God's Word is the only absolute.

It's tempting to dismiss the Bible when its teachings clash with your current reality, but I encourage you to keep reading. Challenge what you've been taught by asking God for clarity. Ask Him to help you see things through His eyes. He is faithful to give us the understanding we need to have confidence in His Word.

As Charles Spurgeon famously said, “The truth is like a lion; you don’t have to defend it. Let it out of its cage, and it will defend itself.”

What God says in His Word is truth, whether we believe it or not. Time passes, societies change, and kingdoms rise and fall, but the Word of God remains the same.

Chapter 9 - Adrian

"The Spirit of the LORD is upon Me because He has anointed Me to preach the gospel to the poor; He has sent Me to heal the brokenhearted, to proclaim liberty to the captives, and recovery of sight to the blind; to set at liberty those who are oppressed."
Luke 4:18

"In all toil there is profit, but mere talk tends only to poverty."
Proverbs 14:23

There are only a handful of people I've crossed paths with in my life who have shown me how to live for God, Adrian being one of them. When I met my wife, the only person she wanted me to meet at the time was her brother, Adrian. I'll never forget how excited she was to introduce me and get his approval. In her eyes, he was the spiritual and parental authority in her life, and rightly so. He is a man of God, family, business, and ambition. I understood why she looked up to him. Being that he was exactly the type of man I wanted to be, I gravitated toward him, asking questions about God, getting marital and parental advice, and even venturing into entrepreneurship.

On several occasions, I accompanied him to minister in prisons. He was the only person I knew who actually did that. I had always heard churches say that was "the mission," and I'd read about it in the Bible, but I had never seen it in action. It's one thing to acknowledge that people are in prison; it's an entirely different level of dedication to set aside a specific day every week to visit them. That kind of commitment is something most people... including myself... rarely exhibit. Whenever I went, I would just sit and listen. Hearing their stories humbled me. They were filled with emotions I knew all too well: bad decisions, regret, being in the wrong place at the wrong time, ignorance, and desperation. I recognized those things because I've been guilty of them myself. In those moments, I saw exactly where my life could have been... and perhaps where it deserved to be.

I realized these weren't "those people"... they were me. They were where I would have been if I'd gotten caught or if the grace of God had not been over my life. I began to see how easily my own decisions could have taken me off course. I am no better than anyone else; we have all fallen short. Let's give grace to those caught in the cycle of bad decisions and work to be the light that guides them back. Many of these men were products of an environment that celebrated its own destruction. They grew up in a culture bombarded by negative stereotypes, one that glorifies fast money and a reckless "YOLO" philosophy. It shows up in every selfie... with a middle finger and a posture of defiance serving as signs of the very mindset that led them there.

"Thus speaketh the LORD of hosts, saying, Execute true judgment, and shew mercy and compassion, every man to his brother, and oppress not the widow, nor the fatherless, the stranger, nor the poor; and let none of you imagine evil against his brother in your heart."

"Thus says the LORD: 'Execute judgment and righteousness, and deliver the plundered out of the hand of the oppressor. Do no wrong and do no violence to the stranger, the fatherless, or the widow, nor shed innocent blood in this place.'" Jeremiah 22:3

"The LORD watches over the strangers; He relieves the fatherless and the widow. But the way of the wicked He turns upside down." Psalms 146:9

With so many verses giving us insight into God's heart for strangers, orphans, and widows, how do we move on as if their lives are less important? Three-fourths of the people whom God Himself highlighted for us to look after are in prison. We should do better... I will do better.

Another attribute I learned from Adrian is diligence... doing what you say you're going to do now rather than later. Procrastination is something I honestly still struggle with. Letting fear of the unknown halt my progress and smother my ambitions, I spend too much time analyzing situations that I end up doing nothing at all. Not being able to act on opportunities when they present themselves has been my kryptonite. I'm a man of many ideas but low execution, and it's costing me, my family, and the people I could have helped in the process.

Here is a list of my personal ideas that I have yet to complete and some that never saw the light of day:

- Seywurd Clothing (Urban Christian apparel)
- Humble Bum Clothing Brand
- Good Man Clothing Brand
- Dad'll Work Woodworking Services
- Dad'll Fixit Handyman Services
- Dad'll Fly Drone Services
- Psalms of Stephen (unfinished book)
- Freddy the Flying Fish (unfinished children's book)
- Seywurd Podcast
- To Be A Good Man Podcast

This book was even an idea I received at least 10 years ago. I just STARTED writing it in July 2025.

When Scripture tells us, "*Be diligent to know the state of your flocks, and attend to your herds,*" I take it to mean we must pay close attention to our own situation and manage what has been entrusted to us. We must take an honest inventory of our gifts, skills, strengths, and weaknesses. Be mindful of the company you keep and the people you allow access to your life. What are your vices, your addictions, or your idols? Where is your time being spent? What challenges are you facing, and who is counseling you through them? More importantly, where do they get their counsel?

When we take inventory of our lives, we begin to see a clearer picture of our place in the world. Often, we start to see God's hand moving, but we also see the things that are siphoning the life out of us. Whatever you water will grow, whether it is to your benefit or your demise. If you find things within yourself that are not conducive to who you are in Christ... or to the vision you have for your family, business, and purpose... you have to let them go. The Bible puts it plainly: ***"If your eye causes you to sin, pluck it out."*** In other words, if something attached to you is weighing you down or leading you astray, get rid of it. Replace those toxic habits with a mindset that contributes to your growth.

Looking back at the businesses I started but didn't see through is a sobering testament to the unfinished chapters in my life. Yet, I remain hopeful because I still have the clarity to see where I need help, the wisdom to accept good counsel, and the willingness to change. I struggle daily to become the man God called me to be, but I have no Plan B. Either I fulfill His purpose for my life, or I become another tragic story; there is no in-between. When I see how Adrian operates... tackling tasks the moment they are presented... it motivates me. That drive

seems to come naturally to him, much like it did for his father, my father-in-law.
If you mention to "Pops" that you need to go to the store, he's on his feet, ready to move right then and there. Several of his children carry that same spark.

I've realized that if self-motivation, ambition, and a sense of urgency aren't in your DNA, you have to intentionally purpose yourself to build those traits from the ground up.

"He who has a slack hand becomes poor,
but the hand of the diligent makes rich." -Proverbs 10:4

"The soul of a lazy man desires and has nothing,
but the soul of the diligent shall be made rich." -Proverbs 13:4

Chapter 10 - Vito & Brick

"Therefore we do not lose heart. Even though our outward man is perishing, yet the inward man is being renewed day by day. For our light affliction, which is but for a moment, is working for us a far more exceeding and eternal weight of glory, while we do not look at the things which are seen, but at the things which are not seen. For the things which are seen are temporary, but the things which are not seen are eternal." -2 Corinthians 4:16-18

"Blessed be the God and Father of our Lord Jesus Christ, the Father of mercies and God of all comfort, who comforts us in all our tribulation, that we may be able to comfort those who are in any [a]trouble, with the comfort with which we ourselves are comforted by God. For as the sufferings of Christ abound in us, so our [b]consolation also abounds through Christ. Now if we are afflicted, it is for your consolation and salvation, which is effective for enduring the same sufferings which we also suffer. Or if we are comforted, it is for your consolation and salvation. And our hope for you is steadfast, because we know that as you are partakers of the sufferings, so also you will partake of the consolation."
-2 Corinthians 1:3-6

Vito is another military brother of mine; our bond goes back over 20 years. We stay connected through calls and texts, keeping each other updated on life, family, and work. Talking to him is always uplifting. He is newly married to a beautiful wife, hosts a successful radio podcast, and is surrounded by a solid circle of family and friends. His social media is a reflection of his spirit... full of his smiling face and positive posts, living and loving life even while battling a serious illness. While he isn't shy about sharing his hospital visits, he never does it for sympathy. Instead, he shares his journey to offer encouragement to anyone in a similar fight. Life can "life" any of us at any moment, but it's how we navigate those trials that reveals what we are made of. These moments build character... humility, patience, empathy, and endurance.

In sharing his struggles with a smile, Vito displays a strength and a faith that truly appreciate life and the God who is seeing him through it. We are only truly qualified to speak from experience once we have walked the path ourselves. I could never genuinely encourage someone battling chronic sickness because I haven't faced it. I don't know the pain, the loneliness of a hospital room, the discomfort of the needles, or the mental weight of hopelessness...but Vito does. He is qualified to speak into those dark places because he has survived them. Jesus tells us in Mark 4:17 that tribulation and persecution arise for the Word's sake. When God gives us a Word, the enemy immediately tries to pressure us into letting it go.

The real test of our faith happens in the trenches. If you are afflicted with an illness, do you still believe He is a Healer? Is He still Lord when a marriage is failing or when children are wayward? Is He truly a Provider when the job is gone, the bank account is empty, and the creditors won't stop calling? Is He still a Comforter in the wake of losing a loved one? How could we ever truly know His character without these experiences or the testimonies of others who have walked through them? Don't let your trials distance you from God; let them drive you closer to Him. If you're going through the fire anyway, make sure you get a reward from the struggle. Let your endurance serve as a testimony of His grace because there is someone watching you right now who will need your story to survive their own. We all have areas in our lives designed to cause resistance. Resistance isn't an obstacle to growth; it is a requirement for it. Just as the resilience of iron is forged in the heat of the fire, Scripture says our character is shaped by "fiery trials." These trials reveal our impurities, bringing everything that is not like God to the surface to be exposed and discarded. The refiner knows the process is complete only when he can see his reflection in the metal.

God uses the heat of our trials to expose the things in us that don't align with His nature. Don't fight the fire; allow the Refiner to finish His work until you reflect His image. Be disciplined so you don't prolong the process through resistance. Trust that in Him, you have the strength to endure the heat until the transformation is complete. During the same time Vito was navigating his struggle, I had another military brother, Brick, who was dealing with his own health issues. Initially, his response was the polar opposite of Vito's. Brick sounded defeated and hopeless; in many ways, he had simply given up. He felt his time was near and had resigned himself to it.

For months, I spoke to them both, and the contrast was draining. I always felt uplifted after talking to Vito, but a sense of dread would wash over me before I spoke to Brick. I spent a considerable amount of time trying to pour into him, but eventually, I had nothing left to give. Honestly, I became irritated. Because we had all served together, I felt compelled to lay it out for him. I told him about Vito's situation and the stark difference in their mindsets. I expressed to him how I couldn't continue to listen to him complain; it was draining for me because I had issues I was dealing with myself. Not only that, but all my encouragement was falling on deaf ears. He just sat there in silence. I don't want to sound as if I lacked empathy for

Brick's situation. I love these brothers as if we were blood, and it was that very love that compelled me to speak up. There is only so long you can pour into a vessel with holes before you yourself run dry. Scripture teaches that if you have a fault with your brother, you should address it between the two of you alone; if he listens, you have gained a brother.
At that time, I knew Brick's condition was serious, but I also knew that life and death are in the power of the tongue. Vito's perspective was different because he refused to let his circumstances disprove God's nature. In contrast, Brick had lost hope, and that darkness was beginning to affect everything around him. I began to pray fervently for him... that God would restore his mind and reveal His power. Months later, when I spoke to Brick again, his entire conversation had shifted. He no longer possessed the "woe is me" mentality that had nearly claimed his life. He was different.

Since then, he has moved to a new state, started working, and joined a church. He still faces health struggles, but they no longer define him. I continue to pray that God makes him completely whole before his time here is finished. I believe in prayer. I know it takes a willing mind and heart to overcome some of the things we deal with, but the power to do so comes from God. If he would have kept that old mindset, I don't think my brother would be here today. The prayers of the righteous avail much. We must be in position ourselves to stand in the gap for those who lose hope. We must bear each other's burdens, but in doing so, we can't allow their issues to weigh us down. People don't invest in a sinking ship. All I can do is offer the necessary tools for self-maintenance and point to God for the heavy lifting, but I can't go down with you. Brick chose life, and I thank God for that. I pray his experience helps someone else.

Chapter 11 - Marco

"Physical training is good, but training for godliness is much better, promising benefits in this life and in the life to come." 1 Timothy 4:8

"Haughtiness goes before destruction; humility precedes honor." Proverbs 18:12

I worked with Marco for a few years on an industrial construction site. I was the foreman of the pipe and iron laydown yard, and he was a rigger assigned to assist me. In the construction world, you often cross paths with the same crews even as jobsites change, but I had never heard of Marco. He was a man of few words and always kept a dust mask over his face; it was a couple of weeks before I even saw his full face. Usually, the elite riggers are sent to "the unit"... the high-intensity heart of the project... while the lesser-skilled workers are sent to the yard. The yard is laid-back, tucked away, and far less chaotic than the unit. Because of that, Marco didn't exactly stand out at first, and I didn't know what to expect from him. However, one thing became clear very quickly: Marco was incredibly fit and remarkably disciplined. He arrived at the gates by 6:00 a.m. every morning, coming straight from the gym. After our morning meeting, he would eat exactly ten boiled eggs... every single day. When I finally asked if he ever grew tired of them, his answer was, "I don't even taste them anymore. I just eat them because they're part of the meal plan." Marco's words convicted me. Not since my military days had I seen that kind of commitment... the ability to be so dedicated to growth that you're completely unfazed by the "tasteless" or difficult parts of the process. Every day, Marco was living evidence of my own excuses. While I was talking about "eventually" getting to the gym, he was already there doing the work. I started questioning why I was struggling to do the things I claimed to value. The truth was simple: I lacked self-discipline. Without accountability, my health had slipped, and that same negligence had bled into my spiritual walk. My prayer life and Bible study had become chores I avoided, and my unfinished home projects had grown into a giant I was afraid to confront.

I realized that while God provides the vision for change, we must provide the will to execute it. He showed me who I was; it was up to me to decide who I was going to become. Unbeknownst to him, Marco had become a beacon of everything I needed to do but wasn't doing. His consistency and self-discipline spoke volumes without him saying a word. I remember him encouraging me to start my own fitness journey; he even went as far as giving me a meal plan and an exercise regimen tailored to my goals. It started off well, but then I missed a day, then two, and before I knew it, weeks had passed. I was so disappointed in myself that I actually started to avoid Marco. I didn't want to see him because I knew his presence would force me to face my own shortcomings. When I think back on it, I realize I wanted what Marco had... his consistency, his discipline, his strength...but I wasn't willing to put in the work. And because I wasn't willing to pay the price, I didn't deserve the result. We often do the same thing with God.

We commit to reading more, praying more, or finally breaking off a habit or relationship that isn't serving us. When we default on those promises, we hide. I don't believe we hide out of fear, but rather out of shame. I was ashamed that, as a forty-year-old man, I didn't feel mentally strong enough to simply get out of bed in the morning. Seeing Marco eat those eggs every morning made me feel convicted and judged... not because of anything he said or did, but because of what I *wasn't* doing. I imagine that is how the world often views the church. We can come across as "goody-two-shoes" or "holier-than-thou" simply for doing what the Father asked of us. It's a trick of the enemy: he uses our own imperfections as ammunition to make us resent our brothers. We sever relationships because their consistency is a painful reminder of our own failures. Marco was more than just a disciplined person; he was a teacher. One day, I thought I saw him standing idle while a man named Carlos did all the work. As I got closer, I realized Marco was actually coaching him through the rigging process. He was training a pipefitter to be a rigger. He did the same for a young woman who wanted to be a crane operator. He taught her the ropes, built her confidence, and eventually she was moved to the unit and later hired at a different site to operate a massive crane.

Despite being one of the best riggers I've ever seen, Marco never sought the spotlight. While others withhold knowledge out of fear of competition, Marco found his reward in building others up. He knew his value and didn't carry the pride that often accompanies skill. On the jobsite, we measure a man's strength by what he can move or by his skill, but his true character is revealed by what he's willing to hand off to the next man. The world tells us to hoard our knowledge, protect our position, and broadcast our wins like a trophy. In reality, humility and selflessness are two things that separate a true leader from a "hand." A man who isn't willing to "show the ropes" to the man behind him is not fit to lead. Don't make the mistake of measuring a man by where he's stationed; people have depth and ambitions that you can't see from a distance. Be the man whose consistency sets the standard, but more importantly, be the bridge that helps the next person reach their potential.

Chapter 12 - Dino

"We are pressed on every side by troubles, but we are not crushed. We are perplexed, but not driven to despair. We are hunted down, but never abandoned by God. We get knocked down, but we are not destroyed." 2 Corinthians 4:8-9

I wanted to include my cousin in this book because I am genuinely impressed by him. He raised his son as a single father despite never having a proper example to follow. Some might say, "That's no big deal; women have been doing that for generations." While that is true, this book is dedicated to the men I've chosen to shine a light on, and he is definitely one of them. Aside from our bloodline, Dino was like a brother to me. As kids, I used to spend the night at his house, and the dynamics between our two homes couldn't have been more different. My parents were strict... we were in church all week, and violent music or movies were strictly forbidden. We couldn't even watch the intro to *The Fresh Prince of Bel-Air* because it was a rap song. At Dino's house, being raised by a single mother, he seemed to have more freedom.

I lived with them during my senior year of high school. My aunt was always working, so we either had the house to ourselves or we were out on the streets. He had a Super Nintendo, and we'd spend those nights smoking weed, playing *Mario Kart* until the sun came up, and listening to "Crossroads" on repeat. With Dino, I got drunk for the first time; I smoked my first joint and puffed on my first cigarette. In my eyes back then, he had it made.

I didn't understand then how much the absence of his father truly impacted him. Looking back, Dino was a natural athlete with a muscular build that most of us had to work years for. He was the fastest of all the cousins, and I truly believe that if he'd had the right guidance, he would have gone all the way in football... maybe even to the league. He played a few years in high school, but one wrong fight landed him in jail, and after that, the path back to the field just seemed to disappear. Foundation is everything. As hard as my aunt worked and as much as she loved him, she couldn't teach Dino how to be a man. There are certain things a boy goes through that require a man's perspective to navigate, like how to regulate your emotions when you're angry rather than letting your feelings dictate your actions; how to swallow your pride when someone tries to provoke you; how to pick your battles; and how to distinguish a real threat from a distraction. These are the subtle lessons... like the importance of looking a man in the eye with a firm handshake... that we typically learn from our fathers. Dino had to learn them from the streets or through the hard lessons of his own experience.

As fathers, we try to prepare our children for the challenges ahead so they don't have to learn the hard way... or worse, never get the chance to learn at all. When Dino became a father, it brought a whole new set of challenges. I can't imagine how difficult it is to try to be something you've never seen... to become the very figure you might even resent. Usually, we hear about men running from that kind of responsibility, leaving the mother to fill both roles. Dino did the opposite. With the mother out of the picture, he anchored himself and did what needed to be done. I watched him pour everything he had into raising his son. Pushing through the loss of jobs, homes, and the lack of support, I saw it take a toll on him. Over the years, he would come to me and share his struggles, and I helped whenever I could, but at the end of the day, he alone was responsible for his child.

We have to be careful when people come to us for help and all we offer is prayer. Don't get me wrong... prayer is powerful...but too often we use it as a convenient excuse to slip back into our own lives, ignoring the real, tangible needs we could have actually met. For men, asking for help or even voicing a problem is incredibly difficult. We're wired to think that if we aren't "handling it," we'll be seen as weak or incapable, but the truth is, the weakest thing you can do is suffer in silence to protect your ego. There is immense strength in setting your pride aside and being honest about your situation or your mental state. My only advice is to be wise about who you trust with that honesty.

"Then the King will say to those on His right hand, 'Come, you blessed of My Father, inherit the kingdom prepared for you from the foundation of the world: for I was hungry and you gave Me food; I was thirsty and you gave Me drink; I was a stranger and you took Me in; I was naked and you clothed Me; I was sick and you visited Me; I was in prison and you came to Me.'" Matthew 25:34–36

I noticed in that verse that Jesus calls those who respond in charity toward people who fall on hard times, "You who are blessed of My Father." In other translations, it says, "You who are righteous." The love, empathy, and kindness you show are a reflection of the Father. We are commissioned to respond in a way that pleases God. Life as a single father was never easy for Dino. Since his son, Destin, is my godchild, I've always made a point to look out for him whenever he needed me. When Destin reached his late teens, he came to stay with me for the summer.

I have three teenagers of my own... twin boys and a daughter... so I thought it would be a great opportunity for him to bond with his cousins. Since we lived in different states, we hadn't spent much quality time together.

To be honest, I didn't know what to expect. It's one thing to converse over the phone...talking about football, school, or girls, but you don't truly know a person's character until you live with them. Dino had always told me Destin was a great kid, but let's be honest: most parents say that. However, Dino was right. Destin was incredibly respectful. His "yes sir" and "no ma'am" weren't just words; they were a reflection of his upbringing. He got along famously with my children. His character was outstanding, and for the duration of his stay, I had zero issues with him. Dino hadn't just raised a son; he had raised a man.

Oftentimes, investing in our children's character is more impactful than providing financial resources. How you treat people, your ability to work with a team, your willingness to be teachable, and even a simple, genuine smile can open doors that money can't buy. These character traits are priceless... and honestly, they're becoming rarer than a college degree. I truly believe Dino gave Destin a solid foundation and placed him in a far better position than he was given as a child. Now, it's up to Destin to build his future on that foundation. In life, we aren't all dealt the same hand, but I believe we all start in the perfect position to fulfill what God purposed for us. If we don't inherit a solid foundation, it becomes our mission to build one for our children... adding to it as much as we can so they can do the same for the generations after them. In the end, honor belongs to the builders.

If you grew up without an example of what a good man should be, training your children to have a solid reputation is the greatest addition you can make to your family legacy. That alone can grant them favor with God and man, carrying them further than any bank account ever could. In most cases, favor opens doors that money simply cannot afford. Teaching our children honor, respect, charity, empathy, patience, and contentment provides them with treasures that can't be bought. A man who possesses these traits is wealthy in the ways that actually matter... with or without a dollar to his name. Dino did an incredible job raising Destin.

Knowing the gauntlet of challenges he faced, many would have expected him to fail or become another statistic in the system. Dino achieved one of the hardest milestones a man can reach: he raised a respectable son despite a lack of resources, encouragement, and the absence of a relationship with his own father. He stood his ground against the world around him, and for that, I will always salute him.

Chapter 13 - Curry & Jay

"For I am not ashamed of the gospel of Christ, for it is the power of God to salvation for everyone who believes, for the Jew first and also for the Greek." Romans 1:16

"Two are better than one, because they have a good return for their labor. For if they fall, one will lift up his fellow. But woe to him who is alone when he falls and has not another to lift him up." Ecclesiastes 4:9-10

Every boy has a place imprinted on his memory that he associates with manhood. For some, it's the aisles of a hardware store; for others, it's a hunting trip or the grease-stained floor of a mechanic shop. For me, it was the barbershop. It was a pit stop for every kind of man... regardless of background, color, politics, or creed. Every walk of life was represented in those chairs. It was a place where ideas were explored and confessions were made without the weight of judgment. It served as a center point for generations, where the elders imparted wisdom to the young, and the youth offered fresh perspectives and social connection to the old.

For seven years, Curry and Jay have been more than just the men who cut my twins' hair. From elementary school to their junior year of high school, these two have shown my sons what it looks like when iron sharpens iron. They don't just provide a service; they provide an atmosphere. The conversations in their chairs are intentional, designed to challenge them and provoke real thought. There is a strategy to fatherhood that involves knowing when to step back. We want to talk to our sons about the big things... faith, women, and the future, but sometimes our "dad voice" gets tuned out. We force the issue or offer advice that they dismiss because they think we're out of touch. That's where the barbershop becomes essential. A barber is neutral ground. They can listen and guide in a way that feels like a conversation rather than a lecture. When you find barbers who walk with God, you know that the seeds they are planting in your sons' minds are coming from a good place. Once, while discussing a situation my father was going through, Curry offered to pray. I agreed, assuming he'd do it later at home or in church, but I was wrong. Right there, while continuing to cut his client's hair, he began to pray aloud. As he prayed, I started thanking God for this man. He showed me that, as followers of Christ, we shouldn't live in a way that suppresses the light He's placed in us. I'll admit, during that prayer, I was nervous. I kept thinking about the other people in the shop. Were they staring? Was this making everyone uncomfortable? But when we said our "amens" and I looked around, everything was normal. No one seemed negatively affected at all. Honestly, I'm not sure what I was expecting. Why was I looking for pushback?

We worry about "offending" a world that is never shy about making us uncomfortable. Curry taught me that day that we shouldn't be hesitant to represent who we are, no matter the setting. Since that day, I've become much more assertive with my faith. I make it a point to be truly present in my conversations, offering prayer for people when a situation is clearly weighing on them. Life hits us all with the same hammers... financial loss, family crises, or the heavy toll of illness and grief. We've all walked through the same fire. As believers, we know exactly who can... and has... delivered us from those afflictions. So let's not be timid about sharing Him with a world that is clearly hurting.

The memories I have of the barbershop as a child are worlds apart from what my sons are experiencing today. Back then, the conversations were mostly street gossip, sports debates, or talk about which schools had the best girls, but Curry and Jay have changed the game. They ask my sons about their ambitions and college plans. They pull out meaningful dialogue and impart insight into the challenges young men face. My boys walk away from those chairs with more than just a fresh fade... they walk away encouraged, energized, and excited about becoming the kind of men they see modeled before them. Be mindful of the men you allow to speak into your sons' lives. Boys emulate what is celebrated in front of them, so you must be the man you want them to become.

Honor good men publicly and show them the respect you expect to receive in return. Boys are always watching, and they are always listening. I see my sons soaking in the conversations I have in the barbershop; they know if I'm being authentic or just putting on an act. They hear how I speak about their mother to people who have never met her. Always honor your spouse in front of them. Never allow your mouth to speak ill of her, regardless of the situation. A boy never forgets how his father treated his mother, and the things you say can never be unsaid.

Chapter 14 - Joseph

"To keep you from the evil woman, from the flattering tongue of a seductress. Do not lust after her beauty in your heart, nor let her allure you with her eyelids. For by means of a harlot *a man is reduced* to a crust of bread, and an adulteress will prey upon his precious life." Proverbs 6:24-26

"Do not let your heart turn aside to her ways. Do not stray into her paths, for she has cast down many wounded, and all who were slain by her were strong *men.* Her house *is* the way to [1]hell, descending to the chambers of death." -Proverbs 7:25-27

The book of Proverbs is a constant warning to stay away from immoral or adulterous women. It's staggering to me that despite verse after verse practically begging us to steer clear, we still see so many men of God fall victim to the same trap. Something must happen to our minds in the heat of seduction. We become willing to throw away our legacy, our peace, and our purpose just for a moment of a woman's attention, her time, or her touch.

Genesis 39 tells the story of Joseph... a man sold into slavery by his own brothers and bought by Potiphar, an officer of the Egyptian Pharaoh. Scripture says that because God was with Joseph, he found favor in his master's eyes. In time, Potiphar made Joseph the overseer of his entire palace; he became a man of great reputation and responsibility. Potiphar made everything available to Joseph, with one exception: his wife.

Joseph was a handsome man, and many women were drawn to him, including Potiphar's wife. She began making bold advances, pressuring him to sleep with her, but Joseph rejected her repeatedly, using God, honor, and even common sense as his shield, and she was persistent. One day, she cornered him alone and tried to force herself on him. Joseph made the only move a man of character can make... he fled. As he ran, she grabbed his garment, and it tore away in her hand. Bitter and rejected, she lied to the guards and her husband, claiming Joseph had attacked her. Potiphar believed the lie and ordered Joseph to be thrown into prison.

This story hits home because it covers the exact terrain we walk as men today. How do we handle being surrounded by attraction when the desire to fulfill it is right there? Joseph tried the logical route first. He explained his boundaries and his lack of interest. You would think a direct "I don't want you" would be enough, but some people refuse to hear "no." So what do we do? As the wife of a man as powerful as Potiphar, she was likely stunning... draped in fine linens and smelling of frankincense and pomegranates. Did her perfume linger in the halls long after she left? Did Joseph have to battle his own heart just to stay upright? What was his prayer in those quiet moments?

We have to be honest: resisting that kind of persistence would be a mountain for any man to climb. Joseph tried reasoning with her, voicing exactly why he couldn't dishonor God, ruin the reputation he had built, or betray the respect of her husband. These were all valid, calculated reasons. It's clear he put real thought into why this act would be foolish... he weighed the long-term consequences against the short-term pressure of lust. We cannot allow what is being presented in the moment to distract us from who we are and what we are called to do, especially when we know that thing is designed for our destruction. The enemy has a way of blinding us to tomorrow by keeping our focus locked on the now. Let me be clear: if you are already entertaining the thought of giving in, you're already caught. Scripture is explicit about what *will* happen to us if we cross that line. The judgment is already set for those who refuse to master self-control. Lust is a powerful drug, and we must take heed, learning from those who went before us so we can overcome these temptations.

When reasoning failed, Joseph tried avoiding her altogether. This sounds simple, but we have to remember: her home was his workplace. That is a difficult needle to thread. It meant staying out of rooms where they might be alone, cutting off small talk, and strictly discussing matters pertaining to the job. He had to eliminate any interaction that wasn't a professional necessity. These steps seem basic, but a persistent woman can make "staying away" feel impossible. A simple glance from a woman is a seed that has toppled nations.

I've seen it myself on the jobsite... women stealing the focus of men working in life-threatening conditions just by walking by. Scripture warns us that "many strong men have been slain by her" and tells us not to "go near the door of her house." Her steps lead to the grave, yet so many men follow like lambs to the slaughter. Needless to say, avoidance wasn't enough. Potiphar's wife caught him slipping. When no one else was around, she threw herself at him, pressuring him to sleep with her while her husband was away. What did Joseph do? He did the only thing left to do: he ran. The sting of that rejection angered her so much that she set out to destroy him, telling a lie that landed him in prison. Even though Joseph made the right decision and was punished for it, God honored his integrity and eventually restored him to his rightful place.

To this, I say: **Run, fellas. Run.** Nothing good can come from that situation. It will destroy your family. You will lose your job, your wealth, your reputation, and your honor... gone.

Proverbs 5:8–11 warns us about the path of the adulterous woman:

"Stay away! Don't go near the door of her house! If you do, you will lose your honor and will lose to merciless people all you have achieved. Strangers will consume your wealth, and someone else will enjoy the fruit of your labor. In the end, you will groan in anguish when disease consumes you."

I'm not claiming the Bible is literally naming things like lawyers, child support, alimony, or STDs but for a man living in today's world, it certainly sounds like it. It reads like a modern-day warning of what happens when you lose your focus. To me, it's saying that the cost of entry is everything you've ever built. Do you really believe the pleasure of a fleeting moment is worth the high probability of losing your entire legacy?

Chapter 15 - Stacy

"And do not be conformed to this world, but be transformed by the renewing of your mind, that you may prove what is that good and acceptable and perfect will of God." -Romans 12:2

I've always been fascinated by the dynamics of the people I grew up with. We often come from the same neighborhoods and the same backgrounds, yet our lives take vastly different paths. I realize that every household is unique; our temperaments and the way we process information vary from person to person. What offends you might not bother me, and how we handle those offenses differs just as much.

But the point remains: at the end of the day, every man is responsible for himself. We all make choices about how we want to live and who we allow to influence us. Whatever path you choose, you alone will reap the consequences or the rewards. No one is more responsible for the man you become than you. A good attitude is a rare find in today's world, and a genuine laugh is infectious in almost any room. Be *that* guy. Be the man people want to be around... the one who is dependable and trustworthy, optimistic, kind, and intelligent without being prideful. Be ambitious, but never at the expense of your integrity. As it happens, that guy is my godson, Stacy. I had the opportunity to visit him at college this past year. He was a junior at Southern Miss, making the Dean's List and newly inducted into his fraternity... fully immersed in everything college life has to offer.

As he took me on a tour, sharing the history of the buildings and the stories behind the statues and stadiums, all I could see was his fire. He was excited about his goals, his courses, and even the adjustments he had to make when things didn't go as planned. It might sound strange, but being around him made me feel hopeful about my own life. Sitting there listening to him, I couldn't help but think, *Man, life is good.*

Society often dictates that if you are a certain skin color, grow up in a specific neighborhood, or come from a fatherless household, you are destined for failure. Some statistics even claim a Black man is more likely to end up dead or in prison before his 21st birthday. The pressure to succumb to "hood norms"... chasing women, dealing drugs, and the race for easy money... is a gravity that pulls hard on those without a plan. Stacy never accepted the stereotypical role he was assigned. He possesses a larger-than-life personality that draws people in, but he remains incredibly selective about who he allows into his inner circle. His mother ensured he was surrounded by a village that pushed him toward his potential, a family that covered him in prayer, teachers and coaches who challenged his mind, and teammates whose camaraderie stretched far beyond the playing field and into their living rooms.

He didn't just survive the statistics; he redefined them.
They say it takes a village to raise a child, and that's true...it has to be the *right* village. It needs to be a community we can depend on to look out for our children when our eyes are away. As a parent of teenagers, I've realized how vital it is to vet the people around my children... their friends, parents, teachers, whoever. We live in a world of diverse ideals, but we must be the gatekeepers of who has access to our lives. However, the strongest influence in the village is the one they see at home. We have to choose our own circles carefully because our children are watching our associations. It is impossible to teach sobriety while practicing excess, or to teach respect for women

while our own talk is full of objectification. If there is a gap between our words and our actions, their respect for us will fall right into it. Our speech must match our walk because children might hear what we say, but they will always mimic what we do.

Chapter 16 - Portia

As I set out to write this book about my journey to become a good man, I always knew my wife played a major role in that transformation. The truth is, I've learned more about my character, my flaws, and what it truly means to be a husband and a father within the walls of my marriage than from any other experience in my life. I met my wife on MySpace. I know I'm showing my age, but back then, meeting and dating online wasn't really a thing. Sure, people "hooked up," but I didn't know anyone at the time who was actually looking for a wife on the internet... and neither was I...But that's how it happened. We exchanged comments online, then phone numbers. After a few weeks of messaging, we had our first real phone call, staying up all night talking until the sun came up. We traded life stories... or at least the polished versions of them. Even then, I was always conscious of the future, wondering if I was talking to my next chapter. At the time, I didn't think so.

She wasn't the "light-skinned, long-haired, half-hood, half-church girl" I had always pictured myself with. She was cute, of a darker complexion, wearing a synthetic wig, and had an online profile summary that actually read: *"I'm the type of girl you can take home to Mama but can still roll a blunt with the best of them."*

I still remember laughing when I read that. Our first phone conversation was... interesting. She had a soft, sweet voice... very feminine, but forward. I felt drawn to her personality immediately. We laughed, shared thoughts, likes, dislikes; everything went great. The longer we talked, the more her persona began to crack. Things she said previously didn't match what she said later.

In one instance, she'd told me she didn't smoke, which was cool because I couldn't stand the stench of cigarettes. Later, I heard her looking for something for what felt like fifteen minutes straight. Being a former smoker, I asked, "What are you looking for, a lighter?" She burst into laughter, and I laughed as well, not realizing that a missing lighter was the absolute least of my worries. Over the course of several phone calls, I found out she was facing serious jail time on drug charges and was even seeing someone else right up until we made things official. Obviously, I must have been partially colorblind because I blew right past every single one of those red flags.

When Portia and I met, I had been celibate for almost a year. I was in a season where I was fresh out of a previous relationship and completely focused on getting my life together. Portia was not in that same headspace. Eventually, our late-night phone conversations shifted into her spending weekends at my place. I went from a posture of not thinking about sex at all to negotiating it. To cope with the compromise, I started playing mind games with my faith. I rationalized that we could have sex, but *only* on Friday nights. In my mind, Saturday was a buffer zone because Sunday was the Lord's Day, and I needed my worship to be pure. It's amazing the kind of contract a man will try to negotiate with God just to satisfy his flesh. Predictably, that flimsy boundary collapsed, and sex went from a Friday exception to our everyday reality.

"But every man is tempted, when he is drawn away of his own lust, and enticed. Then when lust hath conceived, it bringeth forth sin: and sin, when it is finished, bringeth forth death."
James 1:14–15

I knew that whenever Portia came to stay, we would eventually make our way to the bedroom. At the time, I was the only one pushing back against the idea, and as a man, there is only so long you can fight that battle in your own strength. I would give in on Friday night when she arrived, and by Saturday morning, my spirit would be completely vexed. I'd spend the entire day trying to claw my way back to the connection with God I felt I'd just severed.

It was a grueling cycle of pleasure and conviction... a heavy spiritual burden that she couldn't relate to at all. It constantly made me question whether this relationship was truly meant for me. Right in the middle of my journey toward celibacy, I invited someone into my life who fed the exact appetites I was trying to starve.

I began to ask questions:

1. *Did God blind me to those red flags, or did my own lust shut my eyes to them?*
2. *How does a man who claims he "knows what he's looking for" end up so far outside of what he said he wanted?*
3. *Is this God testing my foundation, or was it just me?*

Portia endured some deeply disturbing and traumatic events throughout her childhood and early adulthood. While her resilience was a major reason I chose to love her, that is her story to tell... not mine. All I knew was that I wanted to love her. I wanted to be the kind of man she never knew she would find, or perhaps never even realized she deserved. Looking back, this had to be God. Slowly, the gravity of our relationship changed. My longing to see Portia was no longer driven by physical desire, but by a genuine love for who she was.

Being around Portia made me feel necessary. I felt a new confidence within myself... capable of protecting her, eager to care for her, and secure in my ability to provide whatever she needed. Even though she didn't look like the prototype I usually searched for, she was exactly the woman I wanted to become my wife.

I've always wanted to be married. To me, finding the person you want to spend the rest of your life with was the ultimate goal. As our relationship grew, Portia began to lean on me, look to me for guidance, and ask my advice about work, her mother, and her friends. She was entirely willing to follow me... even at a time when I didn't know the first thing about leadership because I'd never had a reason to lead.

Before her, I was just a single man with no kids, fresh out of the military, with a decent job, reliable transportation, and living out of a FEMA trailer. To say the least, I was content. I didn't want for much, so I had no real desire to climb the corporate ladder or build any kind of legacy. That contentment had made me completely complacent. However, you can't house a legacy in a temporary trailer. Portia's willingness to follow me forced me to look at my life through a different lens. I realized that if I was going to lead her somewhere, I had to start moving myself. As men, we need that. We needed a goal...a mission of some sort. It is hardwired into our DNA to conquer something, whether it's a kingdom, a beast, the admiration of our peers, or the love of a woman. We need to win at something.

I see it all the time on construction sites, in the stock market, and in sports stadiums. We want to catch the biggest fish, drive the fastest car, erect the tallest building, and scale the highest mountain. We need a target. I'm convinced that this is one reason so many men gravitate toward video games. In a virtual world, we can win championships, serve our country, race the hottest cars, or build a criminal empire from the ground up... all in a single afternoon. We get to feel the rush and euphoria that come with victory without any of the physical discipline, disappointment, or real-world consequences that come with defeat.

There are dimensions of manhood that being single simply cannot teach you. Having served my country, traveled the world, and learned to stand firmly on my own two feet, I honestly thought I knew what it meant to be a man. It wasn't until Portia told me she was pregnant that I felt a sudden, fierce urgency to do something more. For the first time in my life, I needed to prepare myself to be someone that others completely relied upon. It was a weight and a pressure I had never experienced. A flood of questions hit me all at once:

- *What am I doing with my life?*
- *What do I actually want to do?*
- *How much does it pay?*
- *Where do I even start?*
- *Can I really be the man necessary to provide for anyone other than myself?*
- *What does that even look like, and how do I make that transition?*

Asking those questions eventually transformed my faith. Out of sheer necessity, I began to run to God for *everything*, and in that desperation, our relationship was forged. I asked Portia to marry me just seven months after we met and shortly after our engagement, we split. That separation was supposedly to give us space to "get ourselves together" and question whether we even belonged together. Looking back, I know that fracture had nothing to do with her... and everything to do with me. My ex and I had been locked in an on-again, off-again cycle for three years before finally parting ways, but a part of me was still tied to her... and Portia's intuition picked up on it immediately. My ex and I had met in a nightclub, but over time, we had both started making our way toward Christ. In the middle of that spiritual shift, I realized I wanted a woman who desired God, and I convinced myself she was the one I would marry. Even though we didn't last as a couple, we kept a friendship alive... even after Portia and I tied the knot.

The problem was that I kept that friendship completely hidden from my wife for years. It was a monumental mistake. The moment you hide something from your wife, you break the foundation of unity. You take a piece of the marriage from an "us" and reduce it to a "you." My ex wasn't our friend; she was my secret. One of the hardest lessons I've had to learn is that secrets have no place in a covenant. The enemy lives in the dark, unconfessed places we try to keep to ourselves. Though I told myself that old friendship mattered, it was really a crowbar prying open a rift in my home. When Portia discovered we were still talking, I hid behind excuses and immediately went into defense mode.

"We're just talking about the Bible."
"It's completely innocent."
"She understands me."

It's amazing how a man will use the Bible to justify his own disobedience. The facts might have been true, but I was completely out of line. The ultimate truth test for any relationship outside your marriage is this: if you have to cover it up, it's because it doesn't belong in the light. The truth is, in the beginning, I didn't think Portia and I would last. I tried to force her into the role of a "biblical" wife using my own flawed understanding of Scripture and what I remembered from my parents' marriage. I was an expert at tracking everything she was doing wrong while remaining completely blind to my own faults.

I constantly compared her to my ex, my mother, and every other woman I felt fit my rigid blueprint of a woman of God. My affection for her began to dwindle. I was anything but a man of God, and the more I demanded compliance, the more she retreated. Three years in, I suspected she was cheating, and months later, I found out it was true. On one hand, I was absolutely crushed. On the other hand, I thought, *There it is...Proof I married the wrong woman.* I began doing mental gymnastics with the Bible, telling myself that infidelity gave me the legal right to a divorce. Because we had three children, I didn't want to leave my kids, nor did I want to tear them away from their mother. So I played the part of the righteous hypocrite, staying in the marriage with one foot out the door, waiting for the next time she cheated so I could walk away with my pride intact and tell the world I had done everything I could. Using Scripture as a weapon to judge her while remaining blind to my own faults was diabolical.

There was nothing holy about my plan to stay just long enough for her to fail again so I could leave guilt-free. Yet that is exactly what I did. That season of my life taught me a lesson:

You cannot force anyone to live for God. The Lord Himself doesn't force His way into a heart, so who was I to think I could police my wife's? The truth was, I barely knew how to obey God myself. I didn't recognize His voice, and I didn't understand how to follow His statutes. So how was I going to manage her life? During those dark moments, I reached out to my ex, venting about everything happening with Portia, myself, and our marriage. It was completely out of line, and I knew it, but my ex became the voice of conviction. She told me, *"You're supposed to be bringing this to God, not me."* She was right. Scripture tells us to confess our faults to one another and cast our cares upon Jesus... not to run around sharing one-sided versions of a story, pointing fingers, and certainly not whispering them to an ex. It's just not wise. Eventually, the weight broke me. I found myself at the altar one night, snot-nosed and crying out to the Lord.

I needed help. I had almost no one in my circle who understood the dilemma of wanting to save a marriage after betrayal. Meanwhile, my pride was screaming in my ear, telling me how stupid I was for staying, how foolish I was for still loving her, and whispering that I should even the score by stepping out myself. My mind was haunted by images of my wife with another man. In my weakness, I started dabbling in pornography and visiting dating sites just to numb the pain. I didn't feel like a man and I felt weak, isolated, and vengeful. It was solely by the grace of God that I didn't completely demolish my covenant. Instead of running, Portia and I both committed to the brutal work of rebuilding our shattered trust. As I began seeking God for direction on how to fix my wife's issues, He only showed me mine. I had to learn that we are only responsible for ourselves. In marriage, though two become one, you can still only control *you.*

My prayers as a husband avail much, but my assignment was to ensure I was being the man God called me to be. Romans 14:4 puts it perfectly: *"Who are you to judge another's servant? To their own master they stand or fall. And they will stand, for the Lord is able to make them stand."* I couldn't make Portia stand, and she couldn't make me stand because that is heavy lifting only the Holy Spirit can do. The reality was, I was barely standing myself. Only God was able to heal our marriage.

Rebuilding trust, restoring communication, and breathing love back into our covenant took real time. I'll never forget my wife telling me that she had to get to a point where she even *liked* me again. We literally had to force ourselves to date while intentionally learning how to enjoy each other's company and find our way back to *true fellowship.* To get there, we had to lay our weapons down, forgive each other, and honestly acknowledge the pain we had inflicted on one another. That meant not just saying the words, but truly letting the past go and refusing to weaponize each other's mistakes the next time an argument got heated. That old cliché, *"Let go and let God,"* became a literal lifeline for us. I was finally able to forgive my wife, work on my own heart, and move forward. For a long time, I took pride in the fact that I had never stepped out on her. I took pride in the fact that I didn't allow her betrayal to cause me to treat her disrespectfully or call her out of her name, but God is not a fan of pride. Scripture is clear: He hates it, and He opposes it.

Therefore, it had to be extracted. He had to force me to look at my own self-righteousness so I could finally deal with it. Throughout the years following what Portia and I call our "*dark years",* I secretly kept in touch with my ex. Every three or four months, I'd send a quick *"U aight?"* text. She'd respond *"yes,"* and that would be it. In my mind, this woman was my best friend, we had history and we knew each other deeply. I convinced myself we could talk about things my wife and I just couldn't. Without realizing it, I had placed the value of that friendship above my own wife.

I kept it hidden from Portia because I told myself it was harmless, but the truth always finds the light. Not only did Portia discover I was maintaining this connection, but she also found out I had visited my ex during a road trip from Louisiana to Texas. To make matters worse, I had her number saved in my phone under a military brother's name. When Portia confronted me with the evidence, my old blueprint kicked in. My initial reaction was to put up my guard, lie, downplay the situation, gaslight, and justify. I was doing whatever it took to protect that hidden relationship, but in that exact moment, a shift happened. I realized I didn't want to live that way anymore. There were no more excuses. In the past, I had convinced myself I hadn't cheated because our connection wasn't physical. Adultery is born in the heart long before it ever reaches the sheets.
I was guilty of looking outside my marriage for an emotional fix, trying to force an ex to fill a void that only my wife was meant to occupy. The definition of an emotional affair is a non-sexual relationship with someone other than your spouse that involves an inappropriate level of emotional intimacy, secrecy, and deception.

Sharing intimate thoughts and feelings outside your covenant creates a bond that undermines and distracts from your primary relationship. That is exactly what it did to ours. Even though it lacked physical intimacy, it was still infidelity. It broke trust and severed the emotional connection between us.

God showed me that everything I was seeking from that woman, I should have been building in my wife. I should have been sharing my thoughts, my fears, and the heavy decisions I faced at home and on the job with Portia. I needed to be calling her throughout my day, cultivating an excitement to see her when I got home, washing her with the Word of God, and praying over her, our family, and our situation. Taking those deliberate steps has been an absolute life-changer for our marriage. I no longer have to look outside my covenant for anything. If you are married, your wife is the ground you are called to cultivate and sow into. The late Dr. Myles Munroe explained this principle well:

"Whatever you give a woman, she will multiply it and give it back to you. You give her a seed, she gives you a child. You give her a house, she gives you a home. You give her groceries, she gives you a meal. In the same way, if you give her frustration, she will multiply that as well. The bottom line is this: if you don't like what you are receiving, change what you are giving."

While I understand there are exceptions to every rule, in my marriage, Dr. Munroe was spot on. During the years when I looked elsewhere for things I felt I needed, the negative emotions I planted in Portia were multiplied right back into me. The moment I started changing my seeds, the harvest shifted. When I complimented how she looked, she took greater care of herself. When I sought her advice, we stayed up talking for hours about everything and anything. When I pursued her heart, she responded with an intimacy I couldn't turn down. Everything I gave Portia, she reciprocated. In many ways, my wife became a mirror reflecting the kind of love I was showing her. Since then, I've completely changed my approach. I shifted how I communicate with her, how I handle disagreements, and how closely I pay attention to her world... her ambitions, her desires, her hobbies, even her favorite snacks.

It didn't matter how small it seemed; I made it my mission to study her. I learned what made her smile, what caught her attention, and what made her uneasy or worried. I started to actually see my wife for the beautifully amazing woman she truly is. I realized that for all those years I spent trying to force her into a mold she didn't fit, I was only making things worse. The moment I surrendered her to God and allowed Him to make the necessary adjustments in her heart, she became more than I ever could have asked for. When I focused on becoming the best husband I could be for her, God made her the best wife for me.

As husbands, it is vital that we take this approach. We may be called to be their covering, but we are not responsible for their actions... and they are under no obligation to follow us if we are not actively being led by God. Watching the Holy Spirit work in the life of my wife is one of the greatest gifts I've ever received. I knew who she used to be. I remember the old habits she struggled with... or flat-out refused to let go of... and many of them are completely gone now. I remember when selfishness was her default, but today she fiercely protects and cares for her family long before she thinks of herself. She respects my decisions even after expressing her disagreements. She follows my lead in prayer, pours into me mentally and spiritually, and has earned the deep respect of our children, serving as the ultimate example of a godly mother to our daughter. I have wept in her arms, and she never once saw it as weakness. She has never weaponized my vulnerabilities against me, and she actively helps me sharpen my gifts. When I couldn't provide financially for our household, she stepped into the gap and carried us, never shaming me for it...not even once. Portia is becoming the type of woman only God can create, and I am blessed to have a front-row seat to witness it.

Chapter 17 - Jesus

"Pray in the Spirit at all times and on every occasion. Stay alert and be persistent in your prayers for all believers everywhere."
Ephesians 6:18

"Why do you call me good?" Jesus asked. "Only God is truly good. [19] But to answer your question, you know the commandments: 'You must not murder. You must not commit adultery. You must not steal. You must not testify falsely. You must not cheat anyone. Honor your father and mother.'
Mark 10:18-19

There is absolutely no way I can write a book about what it means to be *a good man* without naming Yahusha Ha'Mashiach... Jesus the Christ. He is the literal blueprint for walking out holiness and righteousness on this earth. If we want to define what is truly *good,* we have to look at the life He modeled. In Him, we see exactly where our focus belongs. As a man navigating this world, He honored and obeyed His parents, including His stepfather. He possessed a fierce clarity about His purpose, committing Himself to fulfill it even to the point of death. He ruthlessly rebuked anyone who tried to derail His mission, including His closest friends. He moved in absolute lockstep with the will of the Father, doing nothing outside of it.

He stood as a shield for the oppressed, boldly exposed the self-righteousness of those who merely claimed to be children of God, and proclaimed the message of the Kingdom to anyone with ears to hear. Even when His inner circle abandoned Him and denied ever knowing Him because the pressure of the calling became too heavy to bear, He kept going. Scripture shows us exactly how Jesus navigated and responded to every circumstance we could ever face in this life. Yet when we look at the breathtaking miracles He performed... opening blind eyes, walking on water, raising the dead, and even maintaining purity throughout His life... there is one discipline that stands out above them all: His prayer life. Jesus prayed constantly. Before a single miracle was manifested in public, we find Him hidden away in prayer. It was there that He received precise direction on where to go, who He would encounter, what their needs would be, and exactly how to minister to them. Then, at the end of the day, we find Him slipping away once more to pray. It was in those quiet places that He communed with the Father, giving thanks for His guidance, strength, and protection.

Honestly, God is correcting me even as I write these words. Lately, I've been battling anxiety, wrestling with a restless feeling of not knowing what to do with myself. My mind is constantly flooded with thoughts about where I should be and what I should be doing, and I know exactly why. It's because my prayer life is poor. The crazy part is that I know better. The Holy Spirit is constantly pressing on my heart to steal away and pray, but too often I resist. I allow myself to get hijacked by distractions that do nothing to edify my soul. *(Father, I'm sorry.)* I look back and feel as though I've wasted so much precious time, and it is strictly by the unmerited grace of God that I am even able to finish this chapter.

Anyway, your lack of prayer may be the reason you feel stuck. You may be stuck because you have no direction, and you have no direction because you don't have a destination. It may be the reason you are anxious, worried, or afraid to move forward because without a destination, how would you know which way is forward? Do you know where you're going? When we use a GPS, the first thing we do is enter a destination.

From there, the system maps out the route, calculating either the fastest or shortest path. It alerts us to upcoming obstacles and often navigates us around them entirely. If we happen to miss a turn, the GPS doesn't abandon us. It simply reroutes us, calculating a new path to get us back on track toward our predetermined destination.

There are times along the journey when we have to stop, rest, or endure unexpected storms through no fault of our own. Yet, if we know where we are going and stay connected to the system, we can move with confidence even on the toughest roads. We have to remember that we are still heading in the right direction and will eventually arrive. *(Years ago, I had an idea for a T-shirt that captured this perfectly. It simply read: "GosPelS.")*

In prayer, we receive our spiritual direction from the Father. The Holy Spirit dwells within us to guide and navigate our lives toward our true destination, but we must be honest about what that destination actually is. It shouldn't be money, a high-powered career, leading a Fortune 500 company, building a worldly legacy, or even treating Heaven as an escape hatch. Our ultimate destination must be holiness and righteousness... to be made whole, perfected, and cleansed so that we can stand blameless before a holy God. If that is our true target, God will naturally position us exactly where we belong. We are not here to do our own thing and merely string God along until we need a blessing. We have all pursued things... and people... in this life, pouring our time, energy, and resources into them, only to end up empty-handed or completely unfulfilled.

I've loved women who hurt me, and I've hurt women whose company I no longer desired. I've invested time and money into businesses and crafts that I eventually lost interest in, and I've chased jobs that I absolutely hated. It all happened because I stopped communing with the Father. I stopped asking for His direction and started chasing whatever opportunities seemed to make the most sense in the moment. Whenever I hit an obstacle, I would simply think, *Well, that's the end of that,* and drift off toward something else. It was the ultimate symptom of having no destination. As the old saying goes: *When you don't know where you're going, any road will take you there.* Jesus taught me what it means to be *good.*

In the Gospel of Mark, a rich man calls Jesus *"Good Teacher"* while asking what he must do to inherit eternal life. Jesus responds by asking, *"Why do you call Me good?"* and reminds him that no one is good except God. So how can a man be good if no one is good but God? I believe a man can only be considered good if he bears... and is led by... the Spirit of God. It is the sinful nature we are born into that is inherently not good. Yet Scripture assures us that we can put off this old nature through faith in the blood of Christ... the blood that cleanses and sanctifies us so that we may stand before a holy God.

Romans 8:9 tells us: *"You are controlled by the Spirit if you have the Spirit of God living in you. And remember that those who do not have the Spirit of Christ living in them do not belong to Him at all."*

When we are liberated from the control of our sinful nature, we become servants of righteousness, and when we stumble, that same Spirit corrects us through conviction that leads to repentance. Through genuine repentance, we acknowledge that we have fallen short of God's standard. We turn from our own way and submit ourselves to His. It is through this process that we are molded into His likeness. If we claim to be children of God, His Spirit must reside within us. If we are His seed, we must reflect His holiness and righteousness. When our actions, character, and even our deepest desires are led by the Spirit of God, how can a man be anything but good? Jesus also submitted all things to the Father. When facing the horrific reality of the cross, He prayed: *"Not my will, but Yours be done."* We, too, must reach a point where we fully submit ourselves to the ways and commands of God... even if it costs us our lives.

Frankly, I believe the modern church has led countless people astray by teaching that the will of God is automatically coupled with financial prosperity. Scripture is remarkably consistent about how difficult it is for a rich man to enter the Kingdom of God, yet we remain obsessed with obtaining wealth. History repeatedly shows how easily people gain status, riches, or worldly wisdom only to forget God entirely. Why do we think the enemy will not use those same luxuries to lure us away from the Father? If you pray for a house but then drown in stress trying to make the payments, is that God? If the career advancement you fasted for steals time from your family and pulls you away from church, is that truly a blessing? If the person you are dating continually causes you to sin, did God send them?

God's will for John the Baptist ended with his beheading. His will for Stephen ended with him being stoned. The disciples were imprisoned, tortured, mocked, and martyred. Yet we often expect to live our *"best life now."* Where exactly does Scripture promise us that? The goodness of Jesus was rooted in His absolute submission to the Father.

Our goodness is no different. It is entirely dependent upon abiding in Him and walking in His footsteps, exactly as He commanded.

Chapter 18 - Conclusion

Witnessing the transformation of my wife solidified my trust in God in a way nothing else could. Having watched Him change her from the inside out, I am convinced He can do the same for absolutely anyone. No one is too far gone, too broken, or too dirty for Him to clean up and draw back to Himself. I know firsthand what it means to be made entirely new. Today, when I talk to my teenagers and tell them about the kind of man I used to be, it's hard for them to even imagine it. To them, that man is a stranger. I am a completely different person now. I handle life differently. I react differently. I think differently... not only about myself, but about everyone around me. At some point in life, we all have to make a conscious decision about the type of person we want to be when we die. You have to choose whether you will walk the path that pleases God or the path that pleases yourself...You cannot do both.

Lately, death has seemed to be all around us. It has taken family members, people I grew up with, coworkers, neighbors, and public figures I've watched my entire life. Witnessing this, I can't help but wonder where they went. Scripture teaches us that a wise man thinks often about death, and I find myself doing exactly that. I feel like we have forgotten the permanence of the grave. We treat reality like a video game, operating as though we can simply press reset or spawn a new life when this one ends, but there is no reset button.

The life you choose to live on this earth helps determine your eternal destination. Whether good or bad, your reward will be perfectly just.

Let me ask you this:

1. Is whatever you are doing right now worth the reward you are going to receive?
2. Have you ever actually opened the Scriptures and examined the final fate of those who practice what you practice?

Word for word, the Bible outlines the consequences for those who live in sexual immorality, adultery, and fornication. It speaks plainly about those who prey upon the weak, oppress the poor, lie, steal, and cheat. Why do we live lives entirely void of God, yet expect to spend eternity with Him? Why do we believe Heaven is the automatic destination after death? This delusion isn't only believed by the world; it is often reinforced by people who call themselves the church. I know this is a difficult thought, but many of us have loved ones who have passed away, and if we are honest about the lives they chose to live, we may have no scriptural reason to assume they are in Heaven praising a God they never pursued on earth.

Learning about God's mercy, grace, and love should never cause us to take advantage of Him. It should draw us to our knees in reverence. Wherever you find yourself in life, I pray you turn to God through His Son, Jesus Christ. Learn and understand the sacrifice it took to redeem you from the judgment we all deserve. Life is fragile. Every day, people leave their homes expecting an ordinary day and never return. None of us knows when our final breath will come. One day, our stories will be finished, our books will be closed and the lives we lived will be all that remains.

Were they ready? More importantly, are *you* ready? If today were your final day on earth, would you be prepared to stand before a holy God? Are you genuinely confident that you would rest in peace? These are heavy questions, but they are questions worth asking. Tomorrow is a luxury promised to no one. I encourage you to learn about the God who created you and discover the purpose for which you were made. Scripture warns that we will be judged by the same measure we use to judge others.

- Do you extend empathy and grace?
- Do you truly forgive?
- Have you learned to love from a pure heart?
- God requires holiness and righteousness. Do you know what that looks like?
- More importantly, is it found in you?

It behooves us to be mindful of how we treat people and to ensure that we live in a way that is pleasing to God. There is absolutely nothing in this life more important than that. My earnest prayer is that this book serves as a lasting blessing to everyone who reads it. I pray that the Holy Spirit opens your eyes so you can see yourself exactly as God sees you. I pray that you remain vigilant about the company you keep and the subtle influences they have over your life. Ultimately, I pray that you allow God to mold you back into His image and that you fully embody what it truly means to be a good man. The names mentioned throughout this book represent only a fraction of the men who have shaped and influenced my life. In this space, I want to formally extend honor to a few more of them.

In no particular order:

Trace, Preston, Jaleel, Reezy, Joc, Eric, Jermaine, Terrence, Alfred, Ken, Rob, Brian, Mike, Dustin, Brad, Jacob, Randy, Peterson, Hill (RIP), Blu, Doria, Ceja, J. Grey, The Pit Crew, Terry, Dr. J. Smith, Bishop Rankin, Elder Lock, Damon, Chief Wendell, P. Michael, Dody, England, Mark, Kellen, Mr. Don (RIP), Mr. Larry, Lavell, Reese.

In one way or another, every single one of you has left a lasting impact on the man I am today. I love you. I appreciate you. And I thank God for your presence in my life.

Salute.

About the Author

Stephen Merritt Jr. is a devoted husband, a proud parent, and a firm believer in the power of God, the word of testimony, and the necessity of good counsel. As an author and speaker, Stephen's goal is to challenge men to take accountability, reject cultural compromises, and embody what it truly means to be a good man.

Contact:

Instagram
@to_be_a_good_man

Made in the USA
Coppell, TX
04 July 2026

83640689R00056